ABOUT THE AUTHOR

human being

First published 2020.

A catalogue record for this book is available from the National Library of Australia at catalogue.nla.gov.au

Cover photo by Joana Duarte
Author photo by Jack Dekort
Illustrations by Mark De Koning
Book design and layout by Tess McCabe

  Proudly printed in Australia on 100% recycled, FSC-accredited, chlorine-free paper.

ISBN 9780648705710

ziggyalberts.com
commonfolkpublishing.com

brainwaves
ziggy alberts

first edition

PART I.

the writer and the reader

On a glassy windless night
I watched a seagull
meet its own reflection
as it dived into the sea
and wondered why
we find it so strange
to dive into oneself
when seeking
nourishment

trust
trust
trust
trust
trust
trust
trust
trust
trust

In case you've been forgetting

trust.

I can tell you why
it is important
that we have the ocean
it's the only place
where holding your breath
is better than breathing.

One morning
I was trying
to be still
and nearly asked the wind
to not be so distracting
before laughing
at why I might want
the wind
to not move freely
when even at
my most still
breath still flows
and blood still circles

— *natural stillness*

Pause
your narration of everything
and let the world around you
speak

Sometimes,
in rare moments
you get to watch
the earth move
to be an observer,
a reference point
instead of being the traveller,
being still
and seeing that —
even the earth,
just like you
has its own journey
its own movements and stories and reasons
and sometimes
it's nice
being still
to wave and wish it well
as parts of its character
pass you by

— *Trollheim*

It's nice
when the wind
knows where it's coming from
and decides to trust
In its direction

— *commitment*

Should
and could
are very different words
and you should observe
how often
they could be used
a little more accurately.

— *obligations*

Poems
aren't words
they are bridges
not feelings
but directions
because when you are
completely lost
in being
you can't find the words
there isn't room

and I would give everything of it
resign and retire
the ink
the lead
the rubber
the myriads of ways of trying to describe
how it feels

trees would stay standing
and I would note nothing
if I was always
completely and utterly
lost
in being.

Search
and you will never find
what instead
must only come to you.

— *chasing laps around the sun*

At times
I have begged
for my imagination
to not stretch so far
in so many different directions
yet
when I swim
in a sea
where the wind
cannot travel so far
I daydream
about waves.

— *double standards*

If you're ever worried
about being strange
or feeling different
remember—

we live on a planet
with finite lives
where business
takes precedent over
the health of
food water and air
and people work
forty-eight weeks of the year
to afford freedom
for four
for when they retire
doing something
they don't really like
to buy things
they don't really need

and all this is considered
completely normal.

— *definitions*

There will be storms
for this is the sea
and there will be currents
that drag you to meet them
but remember
these currents that swept you
from steady ground
lead somewhere
to a place
beyond turbulence
and if you look past
the turbulence and the currents
to the horizon
It is steady
and so are you.

— *sea level*

How do you feel
offline
and is your dream
about how it looks
or how it feels?

— *hard questions worth asking*

When did
voyeurism
and love
start being mistaken
for the same thing?

Exploring
is completely different
to scrolling photos
of strangers
in an app
that are
only
there
based on
algorithms
of what you have
already seen and liked.

—*inwards not out*

You do not have to make something
into a problem
in order to change it.

I used to feel trapped in the idea
that I could travel the whole world
and still be the same person
I thought that meant
I would never get a break
but now
I think it means that
no matter where you go
when you find yourself
you will always have good company
and travelling
is a wonderful way
of finding new pieces
to the original puzzle

The moon
pulls *whole oceans* of water
in and out
every day
and you're telling me
as a body of mostly water
there is no way
this could ever affect
the ways you are feeling?

You cannot sit
in the warmth of a fire
filled with trees that fell

you cannot walk a beach
of a million broken shells

you,
you just
shouldn't
excuse yourself
from a million examples
of the good that comes
from things breaking
and changing form.

Dreams are not like
to do lists
it is not their completion
or reasonableness
that is important
it's the process
of dreaming itself
that much like living
is most enjoyed
unfinished

The loveliest things
you will feel
in this lifetime
are not in words

the loveliest things
are in the writer
and the reader.

PART II.

adverse side effects to multi-tasking

The day
doesn't really end
the sun just graces
another sea

You should lose your trust
in persons
not people.

—*misplaced blame*

Ziggy Alberts

Our greatest problem
is only in the absence
of many others.

The wind changes direction overnight
why can't you?

—*permissions*

Do not seize the day
seize the eve
before the morning comes
floss your teeth
put your phone down
stretch
write
meditate
do what you promised yourself
tonight
so you can enjoy
the morning
and the day
to come
living well is hard
But living poorly
is harder.

Most of the debris that washes ashore
was already in the sea.
Do we resent the storm
for bringing it to our shores
or be thankful
for now we can see
and address
what was only
out of sight
and just below the surface?

—*emotions like oceans*

*The thing I am most
gravely frightened of
is not experiencing life
As beautifully
as I can express it
in words.*

Sometimes
you need to close your eyes
to see things clearly

— *counter intuition*

To not be busy
is to be still
to not be fearful
is to be brave
to *do not*
is to still *do* something
so instead of us
doing not
let us simply
do.

—*a starting point*

Keep your trials
and errors
in perspective.

Cross that bridge
if
you get to the river
and the water is
moving too fast
to swim.

—*ifs, buts and maybes*

How often
we inaccurately vilify
our thoughts
and how seldom
we accurately vilify
or champion
our actions.

—*not more not less*

Why
do you disvalue yourself
based on
getting lost
in the exploration
of your own thinking?

— *mistakes in judgment*

I couldn't get enough of you
even if I tried
and I do try
and I will keep trying
always
because when I do
it's magic
everything is so clear
when I'm laying in your arms
I just wish
it was more often
and less sporadic
if I do
get to spend
more time
with you
I swear
to the waking sun
it'd mean more
than anything
I could consciously dream of

— *touring's love affair with sleep*

Dream
a million dreams
one
at
a
time.

—*like breathing*

In an evening sky
full of stars
you will catch the shooting ones
despite not being able to see
all the stars
at once.

—*peripheral heart vision*

I have rushed
almost everything
from youth
to embarrassment
getting home
to leaving
arriving on stage
and driving
to get there

I won't rush you.

Today I watched
the sun
set.

How rare
it has become
to do
and only do
just that.

—*adverse side effects to multi-tasking*

To be like water
is often said
to move freely
in a path
of least resistance
but water doesn't do that
water bends around the river,
and breaks the bank
water floats people,
and drowns them
water gives,
but also takes
to be like water
isn't to always be giving
We are water
and to be like water
is to give and take
naturally

—*made of water*

Fall in love
with pictures
and places
moments
and character
pouring rain
and sunshine
the city
and the sea
people
and nature

stop separating
what exists
together

stop believing
you have to choose
one
or the other
to love.

I have been threatened to
go blind
to drown
devoted hours and priority
with zero guarantee
had skin peeled from my back
eardrums burst
wounds that
turned into ulcers
and eyes
that in effort
to protect themselves
grew an extra layer

and not once
did I ever consider
to be without the sea.

That's how you will know
this is how it will feel
to be with her
it's not about
unconditional love
it's about love
regardless of
the conditions.

—*pterygiums*

PART III.

a brief breakup interlude ft. a slightly sad boy

The distance between
the stars above
looks traceable
it looks within
arm's length
like I could cover such distance
the same way
I trace her freckles
mapping her skin
with just my hands.

Then,
at other times,
the galaxy should invite me
to star hop
For that
perhaps
might just be easier
then trying to reach her
even when
she's only at
an arm's length.

I've made breakfast for myself
the way I'd make it for us
and I'm sitting here
crying
I can barely even look at the plate
It doesn't even taste the same
I've made breakfast for myself
because I promised you
to look after myself
but this
it just
it just doesn't make sense
because I've realised
I didn't make breakfast like this
for me
I made breakfast like this
for you.

— *more than half the reason*

The part
that really truly hurt
was today
as I walked up to
the passenger side of my van
to open the door
and you aren't here
but my body
is still completely wired
like you are

When you hold back
in the way you kiss me
what are you saving it for?

*—a question my ex girlfriend asked me about the
only infinite resource available to man*

We should have
washed each other's hair
more often
because your fingers
through my hair
seemed to do a better job
of making
things
clean

—*A woman's touch*

As I walk
the tide line
where salt and water fall
in horizontal cascade
unbound by gravity

I can't help
but see all the shells
you liked to collect
and be reminded
of you

They say you sleep
in the bed you make
but I never had
a good enough reason
to make my bed
until you
were sleeping in it
next to me

—*you made our bed*

Perhaps
a day can be beautiful
and a human can be sad
because
we aren't of the earth
we are delivered here
by our mothers
and maybe
this is our journey
from the arms of our mothers
to the arms of our lovers
to delivering our own

maybe it isn't a return
but a one way trip
along which
the ebb and flow
of the earth and you
slowly become
familiar

—*I've been sad in the most beautiful places*

You just never
fully understood it.
you were
the *one* thing
I didn't have to share
in a lifetime
where I've chosen to share
almost everything
and what I chose
not to share
in writing or public
was all yours.

It was
what was
unwritten and private
that meant the most to me
about us.

I didn't even give us
one night off
where we weren't in a backroom
or in a bus
or surrounded by people

I didn't give
you or me the privacy
to open up
but I expected
myself to have the answer

I naively assumed
you had simply offered me
everything I needed to know
to make a call

like I knew my heart
so well
that in 3 days
I could also know yours
—
I'm sorry.

—Amsterdam   Frankfurt

You gave me
maple syrup
as a parting gift
from your favourite store
and I know
something so sweet
shouldn't make a man cry
but
this 120ml of home
you've offered to me
after our talk
and even though
you are leaving
is so sweet
that it's my chest that hurts
and not my teeth

I'm truly sorry
but there isn't one answer
life isn't that
black and white
to be human
is to make
colours
of everything
that is grey

You do not owe it
to yourself
you do not owe it
to your father
you do not even owe it
to the woman
that birthed you

you owe it
to living
to flowers that bloomed beautiful
despite the conditions
that decided
to break through the concrete
to be a noble part
of pollination and romance
for living
is not
to settle for less
living
is to bloom
or die trying.

—*purpose, higher*

I spend
so much time
being human
and so little time
being

At some point you may have felt
and may feel
like you might be the wrong driver
sitting behind the wheel
and it'd be better
if you stopped driving
altogether

wrong.
do not even entertain that idea.
if you are going the wrong way
do a u-turn
cross double lines
if the road leads to nowhere
patch the tyre check the fluids take a nap
do whatever it takes
then get back on the highway
the car may be temperamental
the route may need to be reconsidered
your driving may need to be improved
but you
are not
the wrong driver
stay in the car
keep the keys in the ignition
and keep driving.

A man who can write beautiful poems isn't the man
who rights his wrongs a man who can sing to
thousands isn't the one to say what needs to be said
a man who can paint highly regarded pieces of art
isn't the man who can draw the line a man who can
cry on a movie set isn't the man brave enough to cry
on your shoulder a man who has a million followers
isn't the man who follows through with what he
promised a man who takes you pretty places and
buys you pretty dresses isn't the man who comes
home from work every day and in hell or high water
tired to the bone washes his hands bridges the gap
stokes the fire and kisses you in a way that proves
he's there for you

that man
doesn't even sit
at the same table
as the man that loves you.
It isn't the same thing.

Being a good man
is a whole other skillset.

I loved
I tried
and I'm going to
keep loving

—*promises worth keeping*

PART IV.

if you listen, the silence sounds lovely

I would accurately describe
human intuition
as the way we saw trees
standing tall and silent
and knew,
unexplainably,
that they would make for
great instruments
and beautiful songs

I watched
a cup of water
start to dance
as music
began to play
and understood
for the first time
what it truly means
when people say
that music
can move you

—*bodies of water*

Being lonely
isn't bad
it's actually
an observation
a feeling
and is seldom negative
if you look at
all the good
that can come
from being
alone.

In fact
you have to be alone
in order
to meet her.

— *I smiled when I realised it was only numbering
afternoons until I was meeting you.*

It's amazing
how often
we believe
the mind knows better
than the heart
when the heart
knew exactly what to do
well before
our mind
had words
to speak

—*heartbeats*

In the busyness
that is between
living and dying
Remember to
water your garden.

Love
is the only pursuit.

Never doubt
the significance
in small acts
of kindness

they are
the tip of an iceberg
in an ever warming sea

Pour her water
open the door
help with the pram
for nothing in return

but instead

the much greater purpose
of re-awakening
the chivalry
that has become
both absent
and daring.

When she moves
through water
she's like a dancer
in a world
where gravity
is her lover
whose affection
she only accepts
when it is
propelling
her
forward

—*the ethereal grace of lady sliders*

Making love
isn't about bodies
when you're really making it
you forget
that you are even a human
in a body
that is separate
to hers
you get so lost
in making it
you find
the beauty of being that is
beyond
and disregarding
of completion

Be a pillar
still and strong
to remind firstly, yourself
and then others
that stillness
is in each of us
and so is the strength
to hold up
your corner
of the world.

— *meditation in transit and public places*

Do not wait
another morning
not one more day
I know
very personally
that the longing
and the searching
the cloudiness
and uncertainty
has become so familiar
it could be mistaken
as good for you
but you
you are on the brink
of discovery
of the unfamiliar and unknown
the self love
and assuredness
honesty and acceptance
I know we are creatures of habit
but if you be brave
and venture into the wild
familiarity
will pale in comparison.
Trust me.

— *6:00am to 6:05am*

Expect there
to naturally be
a certain weight
that comes with living
for at the very least
there is gravity
that we carry
and it's worth carrying
because
the same resistance we face
standing up
also keeps us
grounded.

— *the weight of the world*

At times
I have felt
uniquely apt
at convincing myself otherwise
despite overwhelming obvious evidence
until yesterday
in the morning
with my father
when I realised
we have all declared
the sun rises

when really
the earth turns
to meet the light

— *human traits, section 24, chapter 3: beliefs and
other non-factual habits*

Ziggy Alberts

If you believe
human trajectory
is only loveable
when it follows
a straight line upwards
then why
do most humans
including you
so dearly love
the trees
who's branches reach
nearly as far and wide
as they are tall?

— *tree watching*

Consider yourself
and your internal dealings
a little more
like your navigation
through the world you live within
there are streets you just don't go down
places you don't hang out
rivers that will drown you
deserts too dry
mountains too cold
of both construct and natural state
there is just places and paths and roads
you do not go
out of consideration
for your wellbeing.

We should not think less of the world for that.
We should just navigate it appropriately.
And it's worth learning how
because
there is so many more beautiful places
to explore and enjoy
and we shouldn't let this *awareness*
of such places
change the way we feel
about the immense good within
the only earth we have.

I wonder what is
humans deep aversion
to letting thoughts
simply pass
and simply passing by
the events
of yesteryear.

Instead,
we tend to drag both forward
both into a place of perpetuation
both into a place
they don't belong.

We are obsessed with permission
despite arriving here ourselves
without signing any similar forms.

Amongst all your
striving and good fortune
discipline and goodwill
to be above all that is
the rise and fall
of human tides
you should enjoy being human
as much as possible

the fear
the love
the heartbreak
the hope
all of it

not just because
you are kinda locked in for a little while
but also because
its a hell of a ride
and a privilege to feel
all these many things
that the gods above
can only eternally
envy

— *(I)mortality*

The only thing
that could be
more romantic
then what is meant to be
is the chance
that instead
every path we've walked
every path we've driven
every mistake and good decision
in all of our fumbling and clarity and choice
has led you to me
and me to you
and you and I
embraced in both disbelief
and each other's arms
are entirely responsible for it.

I don't know about you
but I think that's pretty damn romantic.

There is not a place on this planet
that you could go
that isn't missing something
that doesn't have
a but
an if
or an if only
but remember
that isn't what
you are looking for
your home to be
isn't a place
it's a feeling
a realisation
of acceptance
and you will arrive
at the same place in yourself
when you realise
the grass isn't greener
on the other side
grass and home and humans and lovers
are not grown
in the soil
that is not
but the soil
that is.

I think the pursuit of
happiness and love
is much like
sunlight against the sea
you can't stare right at it
or swim to meet it
you will go blind trying
and it's always moving

you can however
observe
where the light is coming from
and what it's reflecting onto
and most importantly
it does not require
your constant searching
in fact
sometimes it's nice
to simply close your eyes
and be guided by the warmth against your skin
to remember and remind yourself:

what you are looking for
isn't how it looks
but how it feels.

Let us go get coffee
and what I truly mean
when I say that is:
let us go somewhere to stop, to appreciate
to excuse ourselves a reason to come together
to converse in a way
that our heartbeats raise
to meet our occasion
let us drink,
then pour
into each other's cup
I don't give a damn how you like it
when it's filled to the brim
or if you have coffee at all
I'm craving the fullness and reminders
realisations and exhalation
the gratitude and satiation
of a cup that is not half
nor filled at all
but instead
the cup that is empty

so now you know
what I truly mean
let's go get coffee

— *refill*

I didn't see the connection between
surfing and meditation
until I realised that
thoughts are movement
passing on through
more or less exactly like
Waves from the horizon
headed to shore
you let some pass by
some almost drown you
some lift you up
some are best enjoyed
shared with friends
and almost all
in the absence of fear
they pour towards shore
day and night
as a natural result of the wind
without your permission and purely as
moments

considering this
I realised
some of my favourite moments in the sea
have been watching waves
and letting them simply
pass on by

— *brainwaves*

Acknowledgements

Thank you to everyone who brought this book to life —
from a bundle of scribbles, notes and musings that it once
began. I've shared these poems with many special people
along the way, and it makes me smile that now those moments
have become a little more permanent. Writing poetry had
nothing to do with publishing it. Writing poetry is what
music was for me at the very beginning: an outpour.
No plan, entirely personal.

This illustration signifies a new and wonderful journey —
just like my first album did back in 2013. *Brainwaves* is another
thoughtfully independent project that was made possible
by my family at Commonfolk Publishing. I'm sorry if any of
the intentional grammatical errors bothered you.
I just really like lower case.

Looking forward to connecting with you all for the first time,
and again.

X,

zig